THE INFORMATIONAL READING SERIES

Michael P. O'Donnell
Margo Wood

New Readers Press
Publishing Division of Laubach Literacy
Syracuse, New York

ISBN 0-88336-323-2

© 1987
New Readers Press
Publishing Division of Laubach Literacy
1320 Jamesville Ave., Syracuse, New York 13210

All rights reserved. No part of this book may be reproduced or transmitted in any form or by any means, electronic or mechanical, including photocopying, recording, or by any information storage and retrieval system, without permission in writing from the publisher.

Printed in the United States of America

Edited by Christina Jagger
Designed by Chris Steenwerth
Cover design by Chris Steenwerth
Cover photo by Tony Potter

Table of Contents

1. Eggs 5
2. The Common Cold 8
3. Clothes Care Labels 11
4. Interviewing for a Job 14
5. What's Happening to McDonald's? 17
6. Motor Homes for Rent 20
7. Caffeine 23
8. Feeding Your Pet 26
9. Snowmobile Safety 29
10. New Help for Deaf People 32
11. Jackie Robinson 35
12. Runaways 38
13. An Athlete's Toughest Challenge 41
14. Hiccups 44
15. Heard a Good Book Lately? 47
16. Electric Blankets 50
17. Men Can Live Longer 53
18. Grooming Your Dog 56
19. Mosquitoes to the Rescue? 59
20. The American Way 62

1. Eggs

Preparing to Read. Why are eggs a good buy?

Words to Know: protein, vitamins, dozen, cholesterol

Eggs have lots of protein. They have iron and vitamins in them, too. Both babies and adults can eat eggs. They are easy to chew.

Eggs are a good buy. They cost less than meat. You can get the best buy on eggs by using this rule. Buy smaller eggs if they cost at least 11 cents a dozen less than the next size larger. For example, if medium eggs cost 85 cents and large eggs cost 96 cents, buy the medium eggs.

Eggs can have white or tan shells. The shell color depends on the kind of hen that lays the egg. Tan eggs and white eggs taste the same, so buy the color that costs less.

Some people need to watch how many eggs they eat. Eggs have cholesterol. Eating too much cholesterol can increase the risk of heart disease in some people. These people should limit the number of eggs they eat.

1. What Did You Learn?

1. What is the rule for saving money on eggs?

_____

_____

2. Does the color of an eggshell make any difference in taste?

_____

_____

2. What Do You Think?

1. Why do you think eggs would be a good buy for someone on a tight budget?
2. Do you think you need to watch how many eggs you eat?

3. **Finishing Sentences.** Read these sentences. Choose the word that makes sense in the sentence and write it in the blank.

1. Eggs have _____ of protein.
   (lots, lets, lost)

2. The _____ of the shell does not affect the taste of the egg.
   (cone, circle, color)

3. Eggs _____ less than meat.
   (cash, cost, cast)

4. Eggs can have _____ or tan shells.
   (white, when, while)

5. Babies and old _____ can eat eggs.
   (point, prepare, people)

6. Some people need to _____ the number of eggs they eat.
   (wash, watch, witch)

4. Word Study: The Endings -er and -est

A. Add the endings -er and -est to each word. The first one is done for you.

slow   slower   slowest

fast   _____   _____

near   _____   _____

cheap   _____   _____

B. Fill in each blank with the correct word.

1. The _____ way to cook eggs is to fry them.
   (faster, fastest)

2. Eggs are _____ than meat.
   (cheaper, cheapest)

3. My house is _____ to the road than yours.
   (nearer, nearest)

4. The smallest eggs are not always the _____ .
   (cheaper, cheapest)

5. A fast food place will fix your breakfast _____ than you can.
   (faster, fastest)

6. The _____ store is six miles away.
   (nearer, nearest)

5. Expressing Your Ideas.

Do you eat eggs? If you do, write a paragraph telling how you fix them. If you don't, write a paragraph telling why you don't and what you eat in place of them.

2. The Common Cold

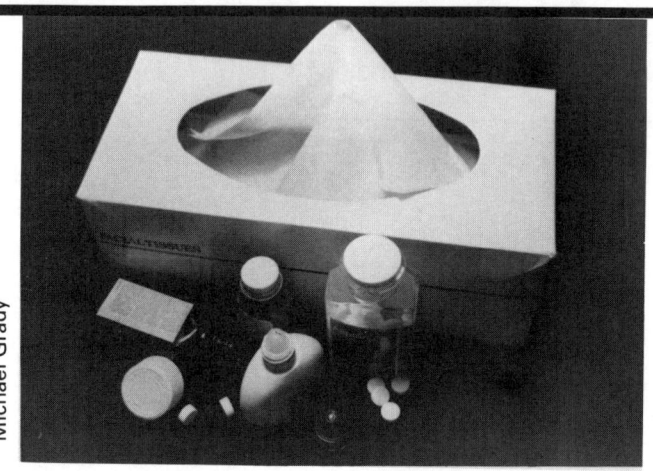

Preparing to Read. What do you do when you get a cold?

Words to Know: germs, viruses, medicine, cough

Colds are very common. Most people have about three colds a year, but children may have more.

Colds are caused by cold germs, or viruses. There are many kinds of cold viruses. When people with colds sneeze or cough, they spread cold germs.

How can you keep from catching a cold? These things may help. Keep away from anyone with a cold. Sleep in a different room if you can. Don't kiss anyone with a cold. Stay healthy by sleeping and eating right. Some people take vitamin C. They say they don't get as many colds.

If you catch a cold, medicine cannot cure it. But medicine may make you feel better. If you have a fever, you can take aspirin. Cough medicine helps if you have a cough. Nose spray helps to clear your nose. Stay warm and dry. Drink plenty of liquids. Take care of yourself. If you don't, your cold may turn into something worse.

1. What Did You Learn?

1. How many colds do most people get a year?

_____

_____

2. Name two things you can do to help you keep from catching a cold.

_____

_____

2. What Do You Think?

1. If colds can't be cured, why is so much cold medicine sold?
2. How does the saying "An ounce of prevention is worth a pound of cure" relate to this selection?

3. **Finishing Sentences.** Read these sentences. Choose the word that makes sense in the sentence and write it in the blank.

1. There are many kinds of cold _____ .
   (viruses, vision, voice)

2. Most people have about _____ colds a year.
   (there, three, then)

3. Cough _____ helps if you have a cough.
   (money, more, medicine)

4. Colds cannot be _____ by medicine.
   (called, cured, could)

5. Not taking care of a cold can turn it into something _____ .
   (worse, worm, women)

6. Medicine can make you feel _____ .
   (better, bitten, butter)

9

4. Word Study: Compound Words

A. Combine these words to make new words.

Example: air + plane = <u>airplane</u>

near + by = _____   every + one = _____

fire + place = _____   after + noon = _____

some + thing = _____   grand + father = _____

B. Use the words you wrote in Part A to complete these sentences.

1. We were worried about my _____ ; he had a bad cough.

2. I plan to see the doctor later this _____ .

3. The drug store is _____ .

4. If you feel cold, sit by the _____ for awhile.

5. When I went to work with a cold, _____ stayed away from me.

6. Even if medicine doesn't cure a cold, people like to take _____ .

5. Expressing Your Ideas.
Write a paragraph telling what it feels like to have a cold. Pretend you are writing this for a person who has never had a cold and doesn't know what one is like.

3.

Clothes Care Labels

Preparing to Read. Have you ever ruined a piece of clothing by cleaning it the wrong way? Did you read the care label?

Words to Know: ruined, disasters, bleach, laundry

Have you ever put a size large sweater in the wash, only to have it come out a size small? Or have you ruined a white shirt by washing it with your red sweat pants? Such disasters can be prevented by reading clothes care labels.

These labels may say *Dry Clean Only* or *Wash in Cold Water* or *Do Not Bleach*. They all serve the same purpose—to prevent laundry disasters!

There is a law that all new clothes must have care labels. The labels must be sewed or stamped on the clothing. The law says the labels must stay on. They must be easy to find and easy to read.

Do you make your own clothes? The cloth you buy must have a care label, too. You can ask for care labels to sew on the clothes you make.

The law can make sure all clothes have care labels, but the law can't make people read them. Preventing laundry disasters is up to you.

1. What Did You Learn?

1. What does the law about clothes care labels say?

_____

_____

2. What can happen if you don't read the clothes care label carefully?

_____

_____

2. What Do You Think?

1. How does the saying "A little neglect breeds great mischief" relate to this selection?
2. Do clothes care labels influence the way you shop?
3. What kind of clothes are the most difficult to care for?

3. Finishing Sentences. Read these sentences. Choose the word that makes sense in the sentence and write it in the blank space.

1. Reading the clothes care labels can prevent _____ disasters.
   (lazy, learn, laundry)

2. Some clothes care labels say *Do Not* _____ .
   (Black, Bleach, Break)

3. Do not wash a white _____ with red sweat pants.
   (ship, start, shirt)

4. If you read care labels, you won't _____ your clothes.
   (run, ruin, rain)

5. By reading the labels you can _____ laundry disasters.
   (protect, press, prevent)

6. Clothes care labels must _____ on clothes.
   (stay, stand, stop)

4. Word Study: Contractions with *is*

A. Read the sentence and look at the underlined contraction. Write the two words that the contraction stands for. The first one is done for you.

1. <u>He's</u> on his way to work.   _He is_____

2. <u>She's</u> a very good cook.   _____

3. <u>It's</u> getting late.   _____

4. <u>What's</u> your name?   _____

5. <u>That's</u> a nice shirt.   _____

6. <u>Who's</u> going to the store?   _____

B. Make each pair of words below into a contraction.

it is = _____   who is = _____

he is = _____   that is = _____

she is = _____   what is = _____

5. Expressing Your Ideas. Describe a laundry disaster that happened to you or to someone you know.

4. Interviewing for a Job

Preparing to Read. What can you do to make a good impression in a job interview?

Words to Know: interview, vouch, argue, dependable, relaxed

Are you looking for a job? You will have to talk to the person who does the hiring. You will have to answer questions. The person will be looking you over.

There are some things that will help you have a good interview. Learn about the company before you go. Dress well. Be on time. Shake hands firmly. Look right at people as you talk with them.

Be ready to talk about your past work. Speak clearly and look interested. Give the interviewer names of people who can vouch for you. Ask questions about the job, but don't ask about pay and time off first. Let the interviewer bring up these things. Don't be pushy or brag a lot. Let the interviewer take the lead. Don't argue, even if you feel like it. Keep cool. The interviewer could be testing you.

Let the interviewer know that you are dependable and that you can work hard. Try to be relaxed. Smile!

1. What Did You Learn?

1. What are two things you should do to have a good interview?

_____

_____

2. What are employers trying to find out about you during an interview?

_____

_____

2. What Do You Think?

1. Do you think first impressions are important in an interview?
2. If you were hiring someone, what would you look for in a person?

3. Finishing Sentences. Read these sentences. Choose the word that makes sense in the sentence and write it in the blank.

1. You can ask _____ during the interview.
   (questions, quick, queen)

2. Let the interviewer know you are _____.
   (depends, distant, dependable)

3. Learn about the _____ before you go.
   (complain, company, country)

4. Don't be pushy or _____ a lot.
   (break, brand, brag)

5. The interviewer could be _____ you.
   (tasting, testing, taking)

6. You shouldn't ask about pay and _____ off first.
   (teen, time, tickets)

15

4. Word Study: The Ending -*ly*

A. Add the ending -*ly* to these words.

Example: slow + ly = __slowly__

sad + ly = _____   part + ly = _____

firm + ly = _____   poor + ly = _____

loud + ly = _____   clear + ly = _____

B. Use the words you wrote in Part A to complete these sentences.

1. If you prepare for an interview, you won't do _____ .

2. You should shake the interviewer's hand _____ .

3. Don't speak too _____ .

4. Look her right in the eye and speak _____ .

5. How you do in an interview depends _____ on how well you prepare.

6. She looked at me _____ and told me she did not get the job.

5. Expressing Your Ideas. Write down some of the things you would say about yourself in a job interview.

16

5. What's Happening to McDonald's?

McDonald's in Freeport, Maine.

Preparing to Read. What does a McDonald's look like? Do they all seem the same?

Words to Know: McDonald's, arches, building, ceiling

Do you know a McDonald's when you see one? It has big golden arches. The building is made of bricks. Its roof is flat with sloping sides. It has a playground and a "drive-through" window. Thousands of McDonald's look just like this, but things are beginning to change.

New McDonald's are being put in buildings that look very different. Some are being put in space-age buildings. The roof appears to be floating. Windows at the bottom of the walls let you see the feet of the customers inside. And windows in the ceiling let customers see the sky.

Other new McDonald's are being put in old buildings that are fixed up. There are no big golden arches. The chairs and tables are old. They may have tablecloths and candles. People enjoy eating in a place that reminds them of the past.

People seem to like the changes in McDonald's. But one thing hasn't changed—the food.

1. What Did You Learn?

1. What changes are McDonald's making?

_____

_____

2. How do customers feel about the changes?

_____

_____

2. What Do You Think?

1. Why do you think McDonald's made all of its places alike for so many years?
2. What changes would you make in McDonald's?

3. Finishing Sentences. Read these sentences. Choose the word that makes sense in the sentence and write it in the blank.

1. McDonald's is beginning to _____ .
   (check, change, charge)

2. The building will be made of _____ .
   (bricks, brakes, boats)

3. Some new McDonald's are put in old _____ .
   (breaking, banking, buildings)

4. The tables and _____ are old.
   (cheer, check, chairs)

5. Customers can look through the _____ and see the sky.
   (winters, windows, writers)

6. People like eating in a place that _____ them of the past.
   (reminds, remains, remembers)

4. Word Study: The Ending -*less*.

A. When an ending is added to a word, its meaning is changed. Add the ending -*less* to these words. What does -*less* mean?

Example: speech + less = __speechless__

age + less = _____   hope + less = _____

care + less = _____   life + less = _____

fear + less = _____   breath + less = _____

B. Fill in each blank with the correct word.

1. The new steel and glass McDonald's left me _____ .
   (ageless, breathless)

2. The old building looked _____ when they began working on it.
   (fearless, hopeless)

3. You would never know this is an old building. It seems _____ .
   (lifeless, ageless)

4. _____ people don't clean up before they leave.
   (Breathless, Careless)

5. The _____ child ran right up to the counter to give his order.
   (fearless, lifeless)

6. Before the new window was put in, the place looked _____ .
   (careless, lifeless)

5. Expressing Your Ideas. Do you think it's a good idea for McDonald's to change its looks? Explain why or why not.

6. Motor Homes for Rent

Chris Steenwerth

Preparing to Read. Do you think you would like to take a vacation in a motor home?

Words to Know: motor home, companies, microwaves, vacation

Did you ever wish you had a motor home? Maybe you can't afford one. But did you know you could rent one? Many companies that rent cars and trucks rent motor homes, too.

Motor homes give you the comforts of home while you are on the road. Some can sleep six people. Many have stereos, TVs, and microwaves. Big ones have full-size bathrooms.

Companies that rent motor homes say renting is a good idea. You can rent a motor home either for a round trip or one way. You can leave the motor home at any of the company's outlets. You can get free, 24-hour road service almost anywhere in the U.S. or Canada.

When you rent a motor home, you don't have to tie up a lot of money. Most companies charge a daily fee. The amount of the fee depends on the size of the motor home you rent. Besides this, you must pay a certain amount per mile. You must also buy your own gas.

If you are planning vacation travel, check into renting a motor home. It may not cost as much as you think.

1. What Did You Learn?

1. What are some things in a motor home that make life comfortable?

_____

_____

2. Name three things that you have to pay for when you rent a motor home.

_____

_____

2. What Do You Think?

1. Why do you think renting a motor home might be better than buying one?
2. Before taking a trip in a motor home, what should you consider?

3. Finishing Sentences. Read these sentences. Choose the word that makes sense in the sentence and write it in the blank.

1. You should check into _____ a motor home.
   (reading, resting, renting)

2. Most companies _____ a daily rental fee.
   (change, charge, chance)

3. You can get free 24-hour road _____ almost anywhere.
   (serve, service, sentence)

4. You can go either round trip or _____ way.
   (one, once, ounce)

5. Besides rent, you must pay a certain _____ per mile.
   (answer, another, amount)

6. You may be able to save _____ by renting a motor home.
   (many, money, month)

4. Word Study: Compound Words

A. Divide the underlined compound words into two words. The first one is done for you.

1. The <u>policeman</u> gave us directions.   _police_   _man_

2. Our motor home doesn't have a <u>bedroom</u>. _____ _____

3. The big ones have a full-sized <u>bathroom</u>. _____ _____

4. A <u>serviceman</u> will fix a rented motor home. _____ _____

5. You can stop at <u>campgrounds</u> on your way. _____ _____

6. Some people get <u>carsick</u> easily. _____ _____

7. My <u>grandparents</u> have a big motor home. _____ _____

B. Combine the words to make compound words.

bed + room = _____   camp + grounds = _____

car + sick = _____   grand + parents = _____

bath + room = _____   service + man = _____

5. Expressing Your Ideas.
Describe where you would go and what you would do if you rented a motor home.

7. Caffeine

Preparing to Read. Do you like coffee and tea? How do these drinks make you feel?

Words to Know: cocoa, caffeine, stimulates, addicted

Do you drink coffee or tea? Do you drink cocoa? Do you drink Coke or Pepsi? If you do, you are drinking some caffeine, unless you buy the decaffeinated form. Decaffeinated drinks have had the caffeine taken out.

Caffeine comes from certain plants. It is found in coffee beans and cacao beans. It is found in kola nuts and tea leaves. Drinks made from these plants have caffeine.

Many people like caffeine because it makes them feel less tired. As one person said, "My morning cup of coffee wakes me up. It gets me started."

Caffeine can also keep people awake. This helps when people have to drive or work late at night. But doctors say that we should not use caffeine in place of sleep.

A little caffeine will not harm most people, but too much can be bad for you. It stimulates your heart and makes it beat faster. It can raise your blood pressure. Some doctors say that too much caffeine may cause heart trouble.

If you have a lot of caffeine, you may get jumpy or nervous. You may get headaches, or you may notice that your face is flushed. Your cheeks and nose may become red. These are signs that you are getting too much caffeine.

How much is too much? Doctors say to let your body tell you. If you think caffeine is bothering you, cut down.

1. What Did You Learn?

1. What drinks have caffeine in them?

_____

_____

2. Why is too much caffeine bad for us?

_____

_____

2. What Do You Think?

1. Why do you think many soft drinks say *Contains No Caffeine*?
2. Do you think caffeine drinks should have a warning label? Explain.

3. Finishing Sentences. Read these sentences. Choose the word that makes sense in the sentence and write it in the blank.

1. Caffeine comes from certain _____ .
   (plants, pleases, pockets)

2. A little caffeine will not _____ most people.
   (house, harm, haste)

3. Too much caffeine may cause _____ trouble.
   (horse, heart, heavy)

4. If you think caffeine is _____ you, cut down.
   (bothering, backing, boring)

5. Many people say that caffeine makes them feel less _____.
   (timed, tired, tried)

6. Doctors say we should not use caffeine in _____ of sleep.
   (please, place, plate)

4. Word Study: The Ending -ed

A. Double the last letter and add -ed to these words.

Example: shop + ed = __shopped__

pop + ed = _____   ship + ed = _____

ban + ed = _____   grab + ed = _____

stop + ed = _____   flip + ed = _____

B. Fill in each blank with the correct word.

1. Some people want the sale of soft drinks _____ in schools.
   (ban, banned)

2. The can of soda _____ over and landed in the chair.
   (flip, flipped)

3. He _____ open the can of root beer.
   (pop, popped)

4. Many people have tried to _____ drinking so much coffee.
   (stop, stopped)

5. The coffee beans were _____ to the U.S. in January.
   (ship, shipped)

6. The baby _____ the cup and spilled the coffee.
   (grab, grabbed)

5. Expressing Your Ideas.
Some people say that caffeine is as bad as alcohol or drugs because we can get addicted to it. Do you agree or disagree? Explain your opinion.

8. Feeding Your Pet

Preparing to Read. What do you think is the best type of food for a dog or cat?

Words to Know: contain, by-products, biscuits, flavor

Dogs and cats need good food. They can get sick if they are not fed right. Pet owners need to know what kind of food is best for their pets and how much food to give them.

There are many kinds of pet foods. Most pet foods are good, but some are not. The cheapest pet foods often contain trash. Their labels say "meat by-products." This can mean that the food is made of animals' hoofs, hair, tails, and skin instead of meat. These by-products have protein, but they are not good for your pet.

Other pet foods are all meat. These may be too rich for your pet to eat all the time. Dogs need meal and biscuits. Cats need dry cat food as well as meat. They also need milk, liver, and fish. Even wild animals don't eat just meat. Most of them eat berries and fruit, too.

Many pets don't care about flavor. They don't get tired of a flavor. Find a kind of food your pet likes and stick with it.

Some owners feed their pets too much. Grown dogs and cats can be fed once a day. Puppies and kittens need to be fed more often. If pets are fed too much, they gain weight. They will not live as long.

If you have questions about how to feed your pet, check with a vet.

1. What Did You Learn?

1. What may the cheapest pet foods contain other than meat?

_____

_____

2. How often should grown dogs be fed?

_____

_____

2. What Do You Think?

1. If many pets don't care about flavor, why do many pet food ads stress it?
2. What kinds of things would you say in an ad for dog food?
3. What do pet owners sometimes do that may make their pets fussy eaters?

3. Finishing Sentences. Read these sentences. Choose the word that makes sense in the sentence and write it in the blank.

1. Cheap pet foods often _____ trash.
   (counter, contain, compound)

2. You shouldn't _____ pet food ads about flavor.
   (because, believe, become)

3. Find a kind of pet food your pet likes and _____ with it.
   (stop, stay, stow)

4. If you need help, _____ with your vet.
   (cheap, chicken, check)

5. Some pet foods have lots of _____ .
   (protein, protect, promise)

6. Even wild _____ don't eat just meat.
   (animals, angry, announce)

27

4. Word Study: The Ending -*ing*

A. Double the last letter and add -*ing* to these words.

Example: hit + ing = __hitting__

get + ing = _____   begin + ing = _____

beg + ing = _____   shop + ing = _____

mop + ing = _____   stop + ing = _____

B. Fill in each blank with the correct word.

1. When you go _____ , pick up some pet food.
   (shop, shopping)

2. His dog is _____ to get old.
   (begin, beginning)

3. Is your dog _____ enough protein?
   (get, getting)

4. I have to _____ the floor after my dog eats.
   (mop, mopping)

5. Some people teach their dogs to _____ for food.
   (beg, begging)

6. Are you _____ at the store?
   (stop, stopping)

5. Expressing Your Ideas. Write an ad for a really good pet food.

9. Snowmobile Safety

Jumping may be fun, but it's not safe.

Preparing to Read. Have you ever ridden a snowmobile? Why do people enjoy snowmobiling?

Words to Know: accidents, windproof, injuries, manual

Riding snowmobiles is fun. It is a fast-growing sport. Each winter more people ride snowmobiles. And each year more people are hurt. In fact, some people die in snowmobile accidents every year. If everyone followed some commonsense rules, there would be fewer snowmobile accidents.

Riders should dress right. Your clothes should be warm and windproof. You should wear good mittens or gloves and good boots. You'll also need a warm hat or a wool face mask. You should wear a safety helmet to protect you from head injuries. Sun glasses or goggles will protect your eyes on bright days. Don't ever wear a long scarf or loose clothes. They could get caught in the machine.

Snowmobiles can break down! Check your machine over before you begin a trip. Carry the manual, a flashlight, repair kit, and a first aid kit with you. Be sure to tell someone where you are going, and what time you expect to be back. Turn back if the weather gets bad.

Be careful where you ride. You must look out for wire fences, fallen branches, and tree stumps. Never *jump* on a snowmobile. If you drive on a road, stay on the shoulder and

29

drive with the traffic. Don't drive on a lake or river unless you know the ice is safe.

If you respect your machine and follow basic safety rules, you can drive safely and have fun.

1. What Did You Learn?

1. How can we cut down on the number of snowmobile accidents?

_____

_____

2. What kind of clothes should you wear when you go snowmobiling?

_____

_____

2. What Do You Think?

1. Why should snowmobilers carry a manual with them?
2. Why do people join snowmobile clubs?

3. Finishing Sentences. Read these sentences. Choose the word that makes sense in the sentence and write it in the blank.

1. Some people die in _____ every year.
   (accidents, accents, acids)

2. You should wear a _____ helmet.
   (safely, safety, softly)

3. Don't ever wear a long _____ .
   (scare, score, scarf)

4. Turn back if the _____ gets bad.
   (water, weather, waiter)

5. When you are riding on a road, drive with the _____ .
   (terrific, taffy, traffic)

6. Respect your _____ and follow some basic safety rules.
   (machine, match, mister)

30

4. Word Study: Words That End with -*proof*

A. Add the ending -*proof* to these words. Study the example before you begin.

Example: wind + proof = __Windproof__

fire + proof = _____   bullet + proof = _____

rust + proof = _____   burglar + proof = _____

water + proof = _____   shatter + proof = _____

B. Use the words you wrote in Part A to complete these sentences.

1. She decided to _____ her car to keep it looking new.

2. The picture window was made of _____ glass.

3. The police officer wore a _____ vest under his jacket.

4. _____ walls between apartments can save many lives.

5. Good locks and alarms helped to _____ the building.

6. When her watch fell into the lake, she was glad it was _____ .

5. Expressing Your Ideas. Would you enjoy snowmobiling? Write a paragraph describing how you feel about this sport.

10. New Help for Deaf People

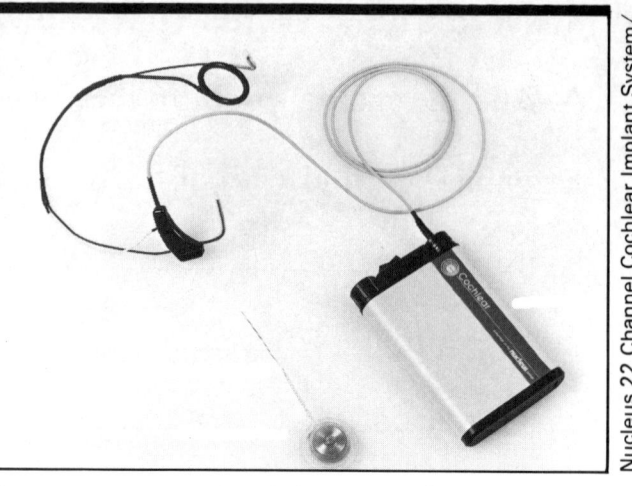

The round artificial ear is implanted in a person's ear.

Preparing to Read. What would life be like if you could not hear any sound?

Words to Know: artificial, electricity, brain, scientists

Think what it would be like to live in a world without sound. You would not hear music or people talking. And you would not hear warning sounds like car horns and fire alarms.

More than 250,000 people in the U.S. are totally deaf. Susie was one of them. When she was two years old, she became very sick. She finally recovered, but she had lost all her hearing. Susie is now eight years old. Doctors recently placed an artificial ear inside her ear. Now she can hear some sounds.

How does an artificial ear work? It picks up sound and changes the sound to electricity. Nerves in the ear carry the electricity to the brain. The brain changes the electricity back to sound.

People who have artificial ears do not hear the same sounds as people with normal hearing. Instead they hear static. But certain sounds cause changes in the static. People learn to tell what these changes mean. They can "hear" bells, sirens, and other loud noises. They cannot hear all the sounds of speech, but they can hear enough to help them read lips. This helps them to understand what other people are saying to them.

The artificial ear isn't perfect yet, but scientists are working to make it better. They feel they have a good start. And Susie agrees with them.

1. What Did You Learn?

1. How many people in the U.S. are totally deaf?
_____

2. What do people with artificial ears hear?
_____
_____

2. What Do You Think?

1. Why is the artificial ear so important to deaf people, if they can't hear words with it?
2. How is a hearing aid different from an artificial ear?

3. Finishing Sentences. Read these sentences. Choose the word that makes sense in the sentence and write it in the blank.

1. Certain sounds cause _____ in the static.
   (changes, charts, charges)

2. Think _____ it would be like to live without sound.
   (where, what, when)

3. The _____ changes the electricity back to sound.
   (broom, bridge, brain)

4. The artificial ear helps _____ people hear.
   (deaf, deep, dear)

5. People with artificial ears hear _____ .
   (state, stare, static)

6. The artificial ear isn't _____ yet.
   (perfect, perform, perhaps)

33

4. Word Study: The Ending -ly

A. Add the ending -ly to these words.

Example: careful + ly = __Carefully__

near + ly = _____   total + ly = _____

safe + ly = _____   normal + ly = _____

final + ly = _____   recent + ly = _____

B. Fill in each blank with the correct word.

1. Until _____ , only a few people could have the operation.
   (totally, recently)

2. Some day deaf people may be able to hear _____ .
   (normally, nearly)

3. The artificial ear can be used _____ .
   (recently, safely)

4. I have _____ found a doctor who can help me.
   (normally, finally)

5. She is _____ deaf.
   (safely, nearly)

6. Now that she has an artificial ear, she isn't _____ deaf.
   (finally, totally)

5. Expressing Your Ideas. Pretend that you are totally deaf. Write a paragraph explaining what you would miss most.

11. Jackie Robinson

Jackie Robinson slides into third base.

Preparing to Read. What makes people prejudiced? How can we deal with it?

Words to Know: manager, Jackie Robinson, leagues, Dodgers

In 1946, the game of baseball was over 100 years old. But there were no black players on any major league teams.

Branch Rickey, manager of the Brooklyn Dodgers, wanted to change this. He started looking for a black player to lead the way. The man had to be special. He had to be a very good player. He had to be brave. Many fans would call him names and boo him. Other players might refuse to play with him.

Rickey finally found his man. Jackie Robinson had been a sports star in high school and college. He was playing on an all-black team when he agreed to play for the Dodgers.

Robinson's problems began right away. Some teams didn't want to play the Dodgers if Robinson played. But the head of the league said they had to. Robinson couldn't believe how much some of the fans and other players hated him. They called him "nigger," "black boy," and worse names. He wanted to fight, but he promised not to. He fought back by staying cool and playing hard.

In his first game, he scored the winning run. He played well all season, but it was very tough. A turning point came when a runner from another team smashed into Robinson's leg with his sharp spiked shoes—a dirty play. Robinson's whole team ran onto the field, ready to fight. They showed they were behind him. He was part of the team.

Robinson played for many years. He was so good that when he retired, he was voted into the Baseball Hall of Fame. He showed everyone he was a hero.

1. What Did You Learn?

1. What did Branch Rickey want to do?

_____

_____

2. Why did Jackie Robinson have to be so special?

_____

_____

2. What Do You Think?

1. Why do you think people treated Jackie Robinson so badly?
2. What can we all learn from Jackie Robinson?

3. Finishing Sentences. Read these sentences. Choose the word that makes sense in the sentence and write it in the blank.

1. In 1946, Robinson was the only black player in the major _____ .
   (leagues, legs, leaves)

2. He could not _____ the hate shown by some of the fans.
   (behave, belong, believe)

36

3. A runner smashed into Robinson with his _____ spiked shoes.
(shape, sharp, shine)

4. When he _____ he was voted into the Baseball Hall of Fame.
(returned, retired, retreated)

5. He showed everyone that he was a _____ .
(heart, haul, hero)

4. Word Study: Adding -d to Verbs

A. The words below already end in *e*. So add just *-d* to these words.

Example: name + d = __named__

agree + d = _____   retire + d = _____

score + d = _____   manage + d = _____

refuse + d = _____   promise + d = _____

B. Use the words you wrote in Part A to complete these sentences.

1. Rickey _____ the Brooklyn Dodgers for many years.

2. Robinson and Rickey _____ upon a salary.

3. Robinson _____ himself he would not fight.

4. When he _____ the winning run, the fans cheered.

5. Jackie Robinson _____ to give up.

6. Robinson _____ from baseball after the 1956 season.

5. Expressing Your Ideas. What makes a person a hero? Write a description of someone you think is a hero. Explain what makes this person a hero.

12. Runaways

Preparing to Read. Why do you suppose that more than a million kids disappear from home each year?

Words to Know: together, disappear, problems, solutions

Todd was 17 and Judy was 15 when they ran away. They said they were in love and wanted to be together. They thought their feelings for each other were special. They thought their parents didn't understand. They decided to run away together and be happy forever.

Two months later, after a long search, a policeman found Todd and Judy at a campsite. They had done surprisingly well on their own. Todd had found a part-time job, and Judy had collected bottles and cans. They were getting by, but they were glad to be found. It was fall and starting to get cold.

Each year more than a million teenagers and children disappear from home. They are not all as lucky as Todd and Judy. About 100,000 never come home. Nearly 2,500 are later found—murdered. The rest just disappear.

The U.S. government helps to find missing children. The FBI keeps records of missing children and runaways in a large computer. When someone disappears, the police notify the FBI. The FBI then sends a description of the missing person to police all over the country.

Running away exposes teens to danger. If teens are thinking about running away, they should talk to an adult they trust. This person may be able to help them with their problems. Todd and Judy were lucky. What if it had been winter? What if they had been attacked or kidnapped? There are better solutions to problems than running away.

1. What Did You Learn?

1. How many children and teens disappear every year?

_____

_____

2. Why is running away dangerous?

_____

_____

2. What Do You Think?

1. What can parents do to decrease the chances of their children running away?
2. Should schools do more to teach children about the dangers of running away?

3. Finishing Sentences.
Read these sentences. Choose the word that makes sense in the sentence and write it in the blank.

1. They _____ their feelings for each other were special.
   (thing, thought, through)

2. A policeman finally found them at a _____.
   (container, campsite, closet)

3. The U.S. government is trying to find _____ children.
   (minor, missing, moist)

4. The FBI keeps _____ on missing children.
   (records, relates, receives)

5. Teens should _____ how dangerous it is to run away.
   (remove, receive, realize)

4. Word Study: Changing *y* to *i* and Adding *-es*

A. Change *y* to *i* and add *-es*. Study the example.

Example: pony + es = __ponies__

fly + es = _____   diary + es = _____

fry + es = _____   penny + es = _____

cooky + es = _____   story + es = _____

B. Use the words you wrote in Part A to complete these sentences.

1. Bill bought french _____ at McDonald's.

2. The teens told the counselor _____ about running away.

3. They wrote about their experiences in their _____ .

4. The only thing they had to eat was a bag of _____ .

5. They picked up bottles and cans to earn a few _____ .

6. Bill waved his hands to keep all the _____ away.

5. Expressing Your Ideas. Suppose you knew a 14-year-old who was very unhappy at home and was thinking of running away. Write a letter to this person.

13. An Athlete's Toughest Challenge

Preparing to Read. Have you ever tried to do something that was very difficult? Explain

Words to Know: athlete, marathon, Iron Man Triathlon

It all began in 1978. Twelve daring athletes in Hawaii decided to give their physical fitness a real test. They tackled three nearly impossible athletic events—all in one day. First they swam 2.4 miles through ocean waves. That's like running up and down the Empire State Building four times while swallowing a lot of salt water! Then each one rode a bike more than 100 miles. To top it off, they ran a marathon. They called these events the Iron Man Triathlon. The winner finished the three events in 11 hours and 46 minutes.

The next year 15 athletes showed up to compete in the Iron Man Triathlon. The winner finished in 11 hours. A woman surprised everyone by finishing fifth. Since then, more and more people have entered the event each year. The winning time has been cut down to 9 hours. So many women compete that the event is no longer called the Iron Man Triathlon. It is now called the International Triathlon.

How do people train for such a difficult event? One athlete, who started out as a bicycle racer, says he went all out to win. He worked with a swimming coach to build up his endurance. He ran long distances and biked every day. All his effort paid off. He broke the world's record for the triathlon by 25 minutes.

Why would anyone want to enter the triathlon? Most athletes say they like the challenge. They like to know they can endure pain and exhaustion and keep on going. They prove they can do something that most people cannot do.

1. What Did You Learn?

1. What are the three events in a triathlon?

_____

_____

2. About how long does it take a really good athlete to complete the triathlon?

_____

_____

2. What Do You Think?

1. Which event do you think is the most difficult?
2. Is finishing a triathlon as important as winning it? Explain.

3. Finishing Sentences. Read these sentences. Choose the word that makes sense in the sentence and write it in the blank.

1. The Iron Man _____ has three events.
   (Triangle, Triathlon, Triple)

2. How do you _____ for such a difficult race?
   (track, treat, train)

3. They tackled three _____ events.
   (impatient, impossible, import)

4. Athletes say they like the _____.
   (change, challenge, check)

5. First they had to _____ through the waves.
   (swim, swan, switch)

4. Word Study: The Ending -es

A. The words below end in *y*. Change the *y* to *i* and add *-es*.

Example: marry + es = __marries__

cry + es = _____   carry + es = _____

fly + es = _____   hurry + es = _____

try + es = _____   worry + es = _____

B. Use the words from Part A to complete these sentences.

1. Every year, Bill _____ to set a new record.

2. After the race, his body _____ for water.

3. She _____ weights when she runs.

4. Every winter she _____ to Arizona to train for the race.

5. When the race is over, she _____ to take a shower.

6. He _____ about swimming through high waves.

5. Expressing Your Ideas. Some people admire those who enter the triathlon. They think these athletes are heroes. Others think the event is dangerous and pointless. They say the athletes are foolish. What do you think?

14. Hiccups

Preparing to Read: When was the last time you had hiccups? How can they be cured?

Words to Know: exception, diseases, temporary, annoyance

Have you ever had hiccups? Did you have trouble getting rid of them? Usually hiccups only last a little while. But a farmer in the Midwest is an exception. He has had hiccups for more than 60 years. He began to hiccup in 1922 when he was helping to lift a 350-pound hog. He couldn't stop. He tried many cures. He went to many doctors. But nothing helped. He learned to live with hiccups, but it wasn't easy.

There are many causes for hiccups. Smokers may get hiccups when they inhale. Laughing hard can also cause hiccups. So can swallowing air. If you eat or drink too fast, you may get hiccups. No matter what causes them, hiccups are very annoying. People want to get rid of them.

You have probably heard of many methods for curing hiccups. Some people think that holding your breath and counting to ten will make them go away. Other people say you should breathe into a paper bag. Others try drinking a glass of water fast or upside-down. Some people think a real scare will cure hiccups.

Doctors tested these methods and found that none of them worked. One other method was tested. This one really did work! Swallow a teaspoon of dry sugar. The hiccups usually stop right away. If they don't, try a little more sugar.

Sometimes hiccups are nature's way of warning us. Diseases can cause hiccups. If you have hiccups often, or if they last more than six hours, check with a doctor. Hiccups may be a sign of illness, but they are usually just a temporary annoyance.

1. What Did You Learn?

1. What are some causes of hiccups?

_____

_____

2. What method of curing them really works?

_____

_____

2. What Do You Think?

1. How do you suppose the farmer's hiccupping has changed his life?
2. Why should you call a doctor if you have hiccups for more than six hours?

3. Finishing Sentences. Read these sentences. Choose the word that makes sense in the sentence and write it in the blank.

1. A Midwest _____ has had hiccups for more than 60 years.
   (farmer, firmer, father)

2. The farmer tried many _____ .
   (cares, courses, cures)

3. No matter what causes them, hiccups are very _____ .
   (annoying, amazing, angry)

4. Some people say you should _____ into a paper bag.
   (break, breathe, bread)

5. Hiccups can be nature's way of _____ us.
   (warming, winning, warning)

6. Hiccups may be a _____ of illness.
   (sign, sing, song)

4. Word Study: Changing *y* to *i* and Adding *-ed*

A. Change the *y* to *i* and add *-ed*.

Example: cry + ed = __cried__

fry + ed = _____   marry + ed = _____

try + ed = _____   hurry + ed = _____

carry + ed = _____   worry + ed = _____

B. Use the words you wrote in Part A to complete the sentences.

1. He _____ many cures for his hiccups, but they didn't work.

2. After hiccupping for an hour, John _____ he might not stop.

3. Every time she eats _____ food, she gets hiccups.

4. His hiccups began the day he got _____ .

5. When she _____ to finish dinner, Jenny got the hiccups.

6. Because the waiter had hiccups, he _____ the tray very carefully.

5. Expressing Your Ideas. Imagine what it would be like to have hiccups all the time. Write about some of the problems you might have.

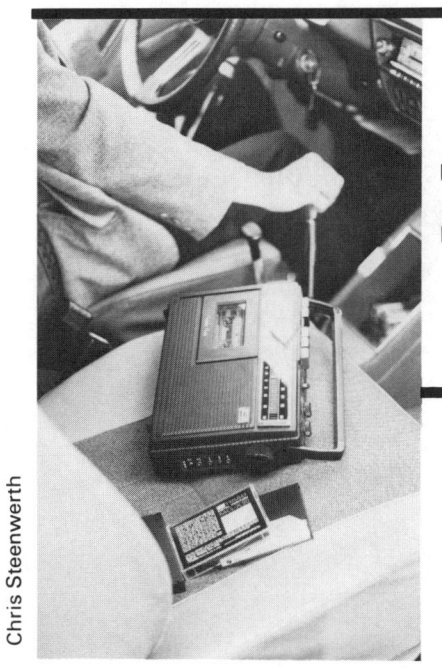

15.
Heard a Good Book Lately?

Preparing to Read. Have you ever listened to a tape of a book while working around your home?

Words to Know: recordings, listen, publish

How can you hear a book? Many people do. They buy or rent tape recordings of good books. At first, taped books were used mostly by blind people; now many others are using them, too.

Taped books are good for people who have trouble reading. They can enjoy good books that they can't read by themselves. Taped books are also good for people who are very busy. They can listen to taped books while they are doing something else, such as driving or jogging.

Taped books are fun to listen to when you have to do a job that doesn't require thinking. You can listen while you are working around the house. It will make the job go faster, and you can learn a lot or enjoy a good story.

Many kinds of books are taped. You can get books to entertain you, such as novels. Other books tell you how to do things. How-to books, such as ones about managing money and getting along with people, are very popular. You can get taped textbooks and children's books, too.

Many companies that publish books are getting into tapes in a big way. Some hire famous actors and actresses to record books. Others get writers to record their own books.

Some people worry that tapes may replace books. Not so, say the publishers. "It's a busy person's market," says one. "There's too much to take in and not enough time. People will still read. But they can listen to tapes while they are doing other things." Tapes may also get more people to read. With tapes, we can use books in a new way.

1. What Did You Learn?

1. Why are taped books so popular?

_____

_____

2. What kinds of books are being taped?

_____

_____

2. What Do You Think?

1. What kinds of books would you like to listen to?
2. How do you think taped books can add to a person's life?

3. Finishing Sentences. Read these sentences. Choose the word that makes sense in the sentence and write it in the blank.

1. Have you _____ a good book lately?
   (head, hard, heard)

2. Taped books are good for people who have _____ reading.
   (trouble, through, terrible)

3. You can _____ to a good book while you are working.
   (listing, listen, little)

4. You can get _____ textbooks and children's books, too.
   (teased, taxed, taped)

5. "It's a busy person's _____," says one publisher.
   (moment, mark, market)

4. Word Study: The Ending -er

A. Add -er to the words in the first column. Since the words in the second column end in e, add only r. The first one in each column is done for you.

tall + er = **taller**   lame + r = **lamer**

fast + er = _____   free + r = _____

clean + er = _____   safe + r = _____

small + er = _____   nice + r = _____

B. Use the words you wrote in Part A to complete these sentences.

1. Listening to a book while you work makes the job go _____.

2. The new, _____ tape recorders fit in a pocket.

3. This taped book explains how to get clothes _____.

4. By using taped books, he is _____ to do other things.

5. Her new tape deck is much _____ than my old one.

6. The tape tells how to make your home a _____ place to live.

5. Expressing Your Ideas. Would you rather listen to a book than read it? Explain.

49

16.
Electric Blankets

Preparing to Read. Have you ever used an electric blanket? Why do so many people like them?

Words to Know: controls, temperature, comfortable, UL seal

An electric blanket is good for cooler climates. It costs only a few cents a night to run. And it is safe and easy to use.

With an electric blanket, you can turn the heat down to 55 degrees before you go to bed. Then you can set the controls of the blanket for a temperature that is comfortable for you. If the room gets cold, the blanket heats up. When the bed warms up, the blanket shuts off. The controls should not be in the warmest or coldest parts of the room.

Electric blankets come in four sizes. You can choose a twin, double, queen, or king-size blanket. Twin-size blankets have only one control. Larger blankets have two. One side of the bed can be kept warmer than the other.

When you buy an electric blanket, make sure it has a UL seal. This means it has been tested and is safe. Also, don't buy an electric blanket for young children or helpless older people. They can't change the setting of the control. They also may get it wet. This could cause a fire.

Read the directions for your blanket carefully. Do not tuck in any part of the blanket that has wires. Check the cleaning instructions. Most electric blankets can be machine-washed. The best way to dry your blanket is to hang it on a clothesline.

If your electric blanket is not working right, turn it off. The label may tell you where you can have it checked. If not, call the store where you bought it. With good care, an electric blanket can last a long time.

1. What Did You Learn?

1. How can an electric blanket help you reduce your heating costs?

_____

_____

2. Why should you look for a UL seal before buying an electric blanket?

_____

_____

2. What Do You Think?

1. What does an electric blanket have in common with a furnace?
2. If you use an electric blanket, where should you put the controls? Why?

3. Finishing Sentences. Read these sentences. Choose the word that makes sense in the sentence and write it in the blank.

1. An electric _____ is good for cooler climates.
   (blank, blast, blanket)

2. An electric blanket is _____ and easy to use.
   (safe, save, sift)

3. When the blanket gets hot, the controls _____ off.
   (shot, shut, shout)

4. The UL seal means the blanket has been _____ .
   (tasted, toasted, tested)

5. Do not tuck in any part of the blanket that has _____ .
   (wires, wears, wars)

4. Word Study: The Ending -est

A. Add -est to the words in the first column. Since the words in the second column end in e, add only st. The first one in each column is done for you.

tall + est = __tallest__   lame + st = __lamest__

cold + est = _____   nice + st = _____

warm + est = _____   safe + st = _____

small + est = _____   large + st = _____

B. Use the words you wrote in Part A to complete these sentences.

1. A king-size blanket is the _____ size you can buy.

2. This blanket has been carefully tested and proven to be one of the _____ on the market.

3. You should not put the controls in the _____ or _____ part of the room.

4. A twin-size blanket is the _____ size you can buy.

5. This blanket doesn't cost as much as some others, but it feels the _____ .

5. Expressing Your Ideas. Some people say they would never use an electric blanket. Other people love them. Write a paragraph about whether or not you would use an electric blanket and why.

52

17. Men Can Live Longer

Preparing to Read. Why do men feel so much pressure? What can pressure do to their health?

Words to Know: pressure, often, compete, healthy

Most men are larger than women. They can run faster and lift more weight, but men often die younger. Why? Some people think men die younger because they have more stress than women. Women also handle stress better than men do.

Most parents expect their sons to be tough and to compete. Sons are taught that they must win. If they are afraid, they are not supposed to show it. They must not be sissies.

Life is hard on men who were brought up this way. They feel that they are under a lot of pressure. They compete for jobs and money. They compete at sports. Some men try to show off. They brag to other men. But deep down, they may worry about losing their jobs. They may worry about failure.

Men think they aren't supposed to cry. They hide their feelings. They don't let off steam. Because of this, they drink more than women. They smoke more. They have more heart attacks and more ulcers.

How can males live longer? Let boys grow up feeling less pressure. Let them play sports for fun. Don't push them into fights. A boy is not a sissy if he doesn't like to fight.

It is all right if males show their feelings. Why shouldn't they cry? Men who can show their feelings are better off. They are better able to care for others.

Men should work at jobs they like. They should also relax and spend more time with their children. They will feel less pressure. They will live longer. They are still men, but they are more healthy.

1. What Did You Learn?

1. Why do women live longer than men?

_____

_____

2. What are two things men can do to help themselves live longer?

_____

_____

2. What Do You Think?

1. Do you think women also feel pressure to compete?
2. What can both men and women do to handle stress better?

3. Finishing Sentences. Read these sentences. Choose the word that makes sense in the sentence and write it in the blank.

1. People who are under less _____ may live longer.
   (strikes, stress, stray)

2. Many parents treat boys _____ than girls.
   (differently, difficult, disrupt)

3. Some men try to show off; they _____ to other men.
   (bring, bang, brag)

4. Men aren't _____ to cry.
   (surprised, supposed, supper)

5. They are still men, but they are more _____ .
   (helpers, heavy, healthy)

4. Word Study: The Endings -*er* and -*est*

A. Add the endings -*er* and -*est* to these words. The first one is done for you.

slow   _slower_   _slowest_

long   _____   _____

sick   _____   _____

young   _____   _____

B. Select the word that fits each sentence.

1. Women get _____ more often than men.
   (sick, sicker, sickest)

2. Men die _____ than women.
   (young, younger, youngest)

3. If you relax more, you may live _____.
   (long, longer, longest)

4. He is the _____ person in his family.
   (young, younger, youngest)

5. My grandmother lived the _____.
   (long, longer, longest)

6. Older people often feel the _____.
   (sick, sicker, sickest)

5. Expressing Your Ideas. Do you agree that most women feel less stress than men? Write a paragraph explaining your ideas.

18. Grooming Your Dog

Preparing to Read. Do you own a dog? What can pet owners do to keep their dogs looking good?

Words to Know: groom, coconut oil, castor oil, lather

Many people have dogs as pets. Dogs look and feel better if they are groomed. Here are several tips to help dog owners groom their dogs.

It is best to groom dogs every day. The first step is to get dirt and dust out of their hair. Long-haired dogs should be brushed and combed. Short-haired dogs should be rubbed with a soft cloth. Never use perfume on dogs.

A dog's coat should be oiled about twice a month. Coconut oil is best because it isn't greasy. Rub the oil in well; then wipe it off with a towel.

You can trim your dog's hair. But be careful not to cut off too much. Dog's hair protects them from insect bites and keeps them warm. Be sure to brush the dog well afterwards.

Most dogs don't like baths. You should handle them gently and use lukewarm water. Your dog's eyes and ears should be protected during a bath. Put two drops of castor oil in each eye. This helps if soap gets in its eyes. Put cotton in each ear to keep soap and water out. Lather your dog well with mild shampoo. Rinse the dog well to get all the soap out. Rub your dog dry with towels, and keep it inside for three hours.

Dogs' nails should not get too long. Buy good nail clippers at a pet store. Your vet can show you how to cut your dog's nails.

Your dog may not like to be groomed at first, but in time it may learn to enjoy all this attention.

1. What Did You Learn?

1. Why is it bad to cut a dog's hair too short?

_____

_____

2. Why should you put cotton in the dog's ears before giving it a bath?

_____

_____

2. What Do You Think?

1. Why is it a good idea to groom your dog?
2. What other kinds of attention do dogs need?

3. Finishing Sentences. Read these sentences. Choose the word that makes sense and write it in the blank.

1. Dogs look and feel better if they are _____.
   (groaned, groomed, grounded)

2. Long-haired dogs should be brushed and _____.
   (combed, calmed, called)

3. Do not spray your dog with _____.
   (perfect, perfume, perform)

4. Dogs' hair _____ them from insect bites.
   (prepares, produces, protects)

5. Buy good nail _____ at a pet store.
   (clippers, shippers, flippers)

4. Word Study: Clipped Words

A. Sometimes people shorten words. For example, they use *doc* for *doctor*. Match the short form of the word in Column A with its long form in Column B. The first one is done for you.

Column A	Column B
gym __gymnasium__	bicycle
vet _____	champion
bike _____	gymnasium
champ _____	telephone
phone _____	veterinarian

B. Use the words from Column B to complete these sentences.

1. Jim took his dog to the _____ when she began to limp.

2. The puppy would not stop chewing the _____ cord.

3. Grooming his dog paid off when it became a _____ .

4. The dog show was held in the school _____ .

5. She trained her dog not to follow her when she rode her _____ .

5. Expressing Your Ideas.
Some people don't agree with the advice given in this article. They feel that it is silly to spend so much time and effort caring for a dog. How do you feel?

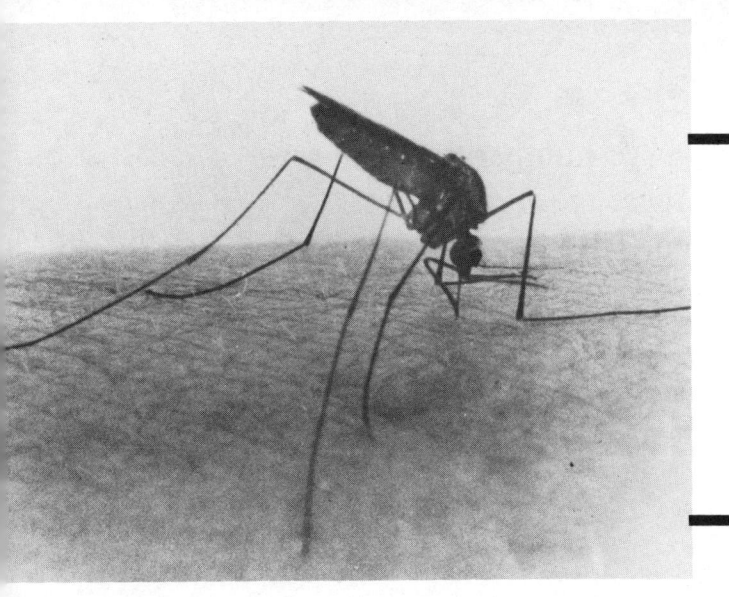

19.
Mosquitoes to the Rescue?

USDA Photo

Preparing to Read. Have you ever been bothered by mosquitoes? What can you do to get rid of them?

Words to Know: mosquitoes, chemicals, scientists, larvae

It's a warm summer night. You are almost asleep. Then you hear a high buzzing sound. It stops. You feel a sting. SLAP! You missed! The buzzing goes on.

For years people have tried to get rid of mosquitoes. They put up screens. They spray bug-killer all over their yards. They buy expensive bug lights. They coat their skin with awful smelling chemicals. But the mosquitoes are still around—and still biting.

Scientists have tried to get rid of mosquitoes, too. They have sprayed the places where mosquitoes breed. The spray doesn't stop the mosquitoes for long. New mosquitoes hatch that are not killed by the spray.

Scientists want to get rid of mosquitoes because they spread certain kinds of germs. Each year, many people become very sick or even die from diseases spread by mosquitoes. If we could get rid of mosquitoes, we could stop the spread of these diseases.

Mosquitoes lay eggs. The eggs hatch into larvae, which look like little worms. The larvae live in water for awhile. Then they turn into mosquitoes. Not all larvae are the same. Scientists have discovered that some larvae turn into mosquitoes that don't bite or draw blood. Instead, they eat the larvae of the mosquitoes that do bite.

Scientists are now trying to raise large numbers of the different mosquitoes. They plan to set these mosquitoes free in places where a lot of mosquitoes breed. They hope to start a mosquito war! Maybe the best weapon against mosquitoes will be other mosquitoes.

1. What Did You Learn?

1. What serious harm can mosquitoes do?

___

2. What is different about the mosquitoes the scientists are trying to raise?

___

___

2. What Do You Think?

1. What problems might spraying mosquitoes cause to the environment?
2. Do you think the mosquitoes that scientists have recently discovered will ever kill off all the mosquitoes that bite?

3. Finishing Sentences.
Read these sentences. Choose the word that makes sense in the sentence and write it in the blank.

1. People put up _____ to keep mosquitoes out.
   (screams, screens, scenes)

2. People also coat their skin with awful _____ chemicals.
   (small, swell, smelling)

3. Scientists _____ places where mosquitoes breed.
   (spray, spread, spring)

4. People can die from _____ spread by mosquitoes.
   (distances, diseases, decreases)

5. Scientists hope to _____ a mosquito war.
   (stand, stare, start)

4. Word Study: The Ending -ly

A. Add *-ly* to the following words.

Example: large + ly = __largely__

calm + ly = _____   slow + ly = _____

fair + ly = _____   year + ly = _____

most + ly = _____   sudden + ly = _____

B. Use the words you wrote in Part A to complete these sentences.

1. When you least expect it, a mosquito _____ strikes.

2. The swelling from the mosquito bite went down _____ .

3. Fighting mosquitoes is a _____ problem.

4. She _____ watched the mosquito bite her arm.

5. Scientists are _____ sure that mosquitoes can be controlled.

6. You will find mosquitoes _____ in warm places.

5. Expressing Your Ideas. Mosquitoes can be very annoying. So can other insects and bugs. Write a paragraph describing which kind bothers you the most and why.

20.

The American Way

Chris Steenwerth

Preparing to Read. Have you ever wondered what it takes to keep our country going for one day?

Words to Know: billion, toxic wastes

Have you ever wondered what it takes to keep America going for one day? Tom Parker was interested in this question. He collected facts about what Americans use each day. He included them in a book called *In One Day*. Here are some of the amazing facts.

- We throw away 200,000 tons of good food every day.

- We junk 20,000 cars and 4,000 trucks and buses every day. They would make a line of traffic more than 50 miles long.

- We use 450 billion gallons of water a day. Almost seven billion gallons of it is used to flush our toilets. That's enough water to fill a giant toilet ½ mile high. The Rose Bowl Stadium could fit inside the seat!

- We throw away 150,000 tons of boxes, bags, and wrappers every day. It would take 10,000 tractor-trailer trucks to haul that much trash to the dump. But it doesn't all go to the dump. Some people don't use dumps at all. They throw a million bushels of litter out of the windows of their cars and trucks each day.

- We gobble up 75 acres of pizza a day. That amount of pizza would cover 60 football fields.

- Each day about 2,450 acres of pavement are laid in the U.S. If we used this much concrete and asphalt to make a bicycle path seven feet wide, it would stretch all the way across the country.

- We make 1.5 billion pounds of toxic wastes each day. If we all shared this, each of us would have to find a way to get rid of nine pounds of dangerous waste every day.

Adapted from *In One Day* by Tom Parker. Copyright © 1984 by Tom Parker. Used by permission of Houghton Mifflin Company.

1. What Did You Learn?

1. How many tons of food do we throw away every day?

   _____

2. How much pizza do we eat every day?

   _____

   _____

2. What Do You Think?

1. Are you interested in reading more of Parker's book? Why or why not?
2. Which fact in this article do you think says the most about the way Americans live?

3. Finishing Sentences. Read these sentences. Choose the word that makes sense in the sentence and write it in the blank.

1. Parker's book contains some _____ facts.
   (amazing, arranging, approving)

2. He _____ what it took to keep America going for one day.
   (wandered, wounded, wondered)

3. They would make a line of _____ fifty miles long.
   (terrific, traffic, taffy)

4. They throw a lot of _____ out of their cars each day.
   (letter, litter, little)

5. Do these facts _____ you?
   (suppose, sunshine, surprise)

63

4. Word Study: The Prefix re-

A. Add the prefix re– to these words. How does the meaning change?

Example: re + use = __reuse__

re + new = _____   re + cycle = _____

re + copy = _____   re + start = _____

re + fill = _____   re + write = _____

B. Use the words you wrote in part A to complete these sentences.

1. Many towns _____ trash by burning it to make power.

2. Her paper was so messy that she decided to _____ it.

3. Many companies now clean and _____ used bottles.

4. We could not _____ the car after we shut it off.

5. The couple decided to _____ their wedding vows.

6. Some people want to _____ the laws that protect our environment to make them stronger.

5. Expressing Your Ideas. Were you surprised by the facts in the article? Do you think Americans use too much? Write a paragraph explaining your opinion.